POSTMODERN ENCOUNTERS

Heidegger ~~and~~
the Nazi~~s~~

Jeff Collins

Series editor: Richard Appignanesi

ICON BOOKS UK
TOTEM BOOKS USA

Published in the UK in 2000
by Icon Books Ltd., Grange Road,
Duxford, Cambridge CB2 4QF
email: info@iconbooks.co.uk
www.iconbooks.co.uk

Published in the USA in 2000
by Totem Books
Inquiries to: PO Box 223,
Canal Street Station,
New York, NY 10013

Distributed in the UK, Europe,
Canada, South Africa and Asia
by the Penguin Group:
Penguin Books Ltd.,
27 Wrights Lane,
London W8 5TZ

In the United States,
distributed to the trade by
National Book Network Inc.,
4720 Boston Way, Lanham,
Maryland 20706

Published in Australia in 2000
by Allen & Unwin Pty. Ltd.,
PO Box 8500, 9 Atchison Street,
St. Leonards, NSW 2065

Library of Congress catalog
card number applied for

ISBN 1 84046 130 6

Typesetting by Wayzgoose

Printed and bound in the UK by
Cox & Wyman Ltd., Reading

A Political Encounter

'Nazism' and 'Heidegger' have been problematic figures in the history and culture of the 20th century.

The former brought into existence a novel machinery of totalitarian government, harnessed to industrial capitalism and modern technology, which within twelve years had murdered some six million people in its extermination programmes, subjected millions more to brutalised slave labour or to forced migrations across and beyond Europe, and in a war of its own prosecution had killed nearly four million troops on the German side alone, while reducing the German economy, its major cities and infrastructures to ruin. The list of indictments, much longer, can at least begin there.

Martin Heidegger, the German philosopher, is problematic for different reasons. In his early work of the 1920s he proposed a radical rethinking of human subjectivity, questioning what it might mean to have one's existence as a 'human being'. In this he rivals other modern, innovating discourses on subjectivity – for example, Freud's psychoanalysis and scientific psychology.

Heidegger also proposed a 'thinking', distinct from 'philosophising', which questioned the foundjations of Western philosophy. In this the stakes are high, since the philosophical tradition in question spans two and a half thousand years. Long-accepted notions of reason, logic and truth, for instance, might no longer be allowed their assurance.

Heidegger had an even more ambitious project: to address the question of being. He interrogated not just human being, but being 'in general', the fact that entities have their existence. He offered to ontology (the grand tradition of philosophical speculation on being) a radically new beginning.

The encounter between Heidegger's thinking and Nazism has been described as disastrous, even monstrous. Metaphors of collision lend themselves: as if in some train crash, perhaps, productive or not, the most innovative philosopher of the 20th century lent his thinking to one of its most notorious political regimes. The encounter between these two, blunderingly aligned or grossly impacted, has had repercussions ever since.

Questions and Issues

Few debates in contemporary philosophy have had as much concentrated resonance. In a sense, 'Heidegger's politics' has become a testing ground for different ways of thinking, an arena with a long history of allegiances, re-alignments and fractures.

4

At least two broad types of inquiry stand out. On the one hand, there have been empirical questions, with competing facts and interpretations. These have often been couched biographically: the facts of the life. What did he do? How deep was his commitment? How long did it last: a couple of years of errancy, perhaps 1933–34, or until his death, maybe unrepentant, in 1976?

Simple facts, as usual, can reverberate with complexities. If we ask 'Was Heidegger indeed a Nazi?', we might also ask how we could assuredly tell. We immediately confront questions with a wider relevance, including what 'being a Nazi' could mean, in various contexts, today.

On the other hand, there have been difficult questions for philosophy, and for anyone now engaging with Heidegger's thinking. Can his philosophical works be read *without regard for* his known political allegiances? Are these completely separate, purely autonomous spheres? Or are there passages or movements between them, points of contact or even structural linkages, which bind them together in some way? And if the latter, should Heidegger's texts continue to be circulated with admiration, as vital resources for thinking?

There is a wider relevance in those questions, too.

The encounter of the 1930s brought together not only a particular thinker and the Nazi Party, but also more generally, philosophy and politics. How might we think of 'the politics of philosophy' today?

These questions, piling up and proliferating, suggest at least something of what is at stake in the 'Heidegger case', and why it has been generating publications for more than sixty years. Colette Audry, in 1934 perhaps the first to raise the issues publicly in France, later put it succinctly:

I have a whole dossier on it; it has grabbed me, I think, because our whole epoch as well as the content we give to the word 'culture' are implicated in it.[1]

As Audry suggests, there are historical implications, but they are not tied strictly to their time.

Postmodern Politics

Some of the fiercest 'Heidegger wars' have been occurring since the late 1980s, and they enter a field of debate over so-called *postmodern* politics. Taking the term elastically, it describes how recent critiques of cultural modernism and socio-economic modernity have been put to use in political territories.

Most dramatically, the postmodern critics have set

their sights on totalising discourses that work to eradicate social and cultural differences. Essentialisms of class, ethnicity or gender, and exclusionary thinking of many kinds, have also been targets. In various guises, such as neo- or post- Feminisms and Marxisms, post-colonial politics and counter-cultural movements, a radical re-framing of traditional politics has been proposed.

Within these fields, a now-familiar list of names has been circulated: Jean-François Lyotard, Jacques Derrida, Gilles Deleuze, Michel Foucault, Jacques Lacan and others – thinkers often categorised as post-structuralist. They have proposed radical changes in the ways we think about knowledge, power, subjectivity and language, and in various and distinct ways they have advocated counter-philosophies, anti-essentialisms, anti-foundation-alisms and strategies of deconstruction. And here the figure of Heidegger enters. His critique of subjectivity, his 'thinking otherwise' to Western tradition, even his question of being, have proved significant and useful to many post-structuralists.

From some quarters, though, there have been charges of irrationalism and political irresponsibility. Post-structuralists have been held to reject reasoned, grounded discourse, and all stable categories for normative judgement and purposeful action.[2] These objections have a political edge. How can post-structuralists successfully oppose the forces of domination and oppression, whether these arrive in intensified global capitalism, state authoritarianism, militarisms and nationalisms, forms of patriarchy or religious fundamentalism, or maybe in other forms? And to drive the criticisms home, these thinkers allow the influence of a philosopher, Heidegger, enthusiastic for Nazism.

The perspective that informs this book is rather different. It suggests that both the biographical facts and the philosophical critiques of Heidegger's politics need to be taken seriously. There are practical politics that demand it – forms of 'conservative revolution' and of New Right populism have taken a deep hold recently in Western-type societies, and the latter have no impregnable barriers against resurgent neo-Nazisms or emergent totalitarianisms.

It might also turn out, though, that any possibility of approaching democracy and social justice depends on a willingness to think about thinking, and to disturb the usual taken-for-granted categories of political practice. Heidegger's texts might play a part in this – or so some of his supporters have argued.

We deal, then, with quite a difficult conundrum: how texts by a philosopher who advocated Nazism might lend themselves, even in seemingly paradoxical torsion, to political struggles that *resist* Nazisms of all kinds. That is the book's main question. It considers especially the contribution made by Jacques Derrida, whose treatments of condemnatory discourse, Nazism's borders and political ethics are perhaps the most startling use of Heidegger against his own avowed politics. Along with other contributors, Derrida has proposed a radical re-thinking of what we can mean by totalitarianism and democracy. First, though, what has been known of Heidegger's politics?

Silences and Separations

Depending on its route, a first circuit of inquiry might yield little or nothing. Take, as an example, Heidegger's first collected essays to be translated into English (*Existence and Being*, published in 1949), which offered on matters of politics little more than editor Werner Brock's announcement that Heidegger was Rector of Freiburg University from 1933 to 1934, 'under the National Socialist regime'.[3] The economy of the statement, and its tiny hint of duress, deflects questions of politics. That will not be a path of thinking for anyone who is thinking with Heidegger.

Given the critiques that began to be produced in post-war Germany, a semi-biographical study by Walter Biemel in 1973 was obliged to go further. It presents Heidegger's life as devoid of 'capricious occurrences', comparable even to Kant's life of 'outward monotony and uniformity'. But there is a veiled reference to an unspecified 'political error':

The political error of 1933 was of short duration . . . It is superficial to pounce on it in order to discredit Heidegger. Had the error been a result of his philosophical thought, this thinking itself would have come to an end with the correction of the error. What actually happened was just the opposite, for it was after 1934 that his thinking really began to unfold. His long years of university teaching were devoted solely to the task of communicating his experience of thinking.[4]

So to anyone who could identify the error, three reassurances are offered: it was short-lived, it was corrected, it was not tied to Heidegger's thinking.

These have been the most common stances of Heidegger's supporters. If a silence of some kind seems inadequate, as in a biographical account, then the issues are rendered insignificant or marginalised. Ultimately, the philosophy is ring-fenced: biographers or historians might address Heidegger's politics, but they are of no concern to any proper philosopher. Jürgen Habermas, Frankfurt School Marxist, has described the effect this can have. As a student from 1949 to 1954 he was powerfully influenced by Heidegger's philosophy, and his two dissertation tutors had both been strong supporters of Hitler's revolution.

Nobody told us about their past. We had to find out step by step for ourselves. It took me four years of studies, mostly just accidentally looking into books in libraries, to discover what they had been thinking only a decade or a decade and a half ago. Think what that meant![5]

But should we demand a discourse on politics every time a text by Heidegger is circulated or discussed? Where do we stop? A black star of some kind, or protocols or prefaces of rejection, as with some post-war editions of *Mein Kampf*: please don't read this? The difficulty is that Heidegger's philosophy has had a huge impact in 20th-century thought, and the maybe incalculable impact of eugenic-racist Nazism is still with us. A demand does arise – both ethically and politically – and tactful silences will not address it.

Freiburg, 1933

What was the 'error'? A *prima facie* case: Heidegger lent his public support to Hitler's party in the 1930s. The facts of the case gravitate around his term of office as Rector of Freiburg University, its chief administrative position. Heidegger, born 1889 and university trained from 1909 to 1915, was by then a philosopher with a growing reputation for innovative syntheses of ancient, medieval and modern philosophy.

After his election as Rector in April 1933, he joined the National Socialist Party. His inaugural address to the university in May 1933 unequivocally valorised the Party and its leader – as did his other public speeches and publications in newspapers, Party journals and student newsheets between 1933 and 1934. In October 1933, he was re-inaugurated as one of Hitler's new non-elected 'leader-rectors'.

The events belong chronologically to the first two years of National Socialist rule in Germany, from January 1933. Heidegger was not alone in his enthusiasm, as Party vote shares suggest: 2.6 per cent in 1928; and 43.9 per cent in March 1933.

He could not have been unaware of the rapid moves to establish a single-party, anti-Communist state with racist policies. In February 1933, the Reichstag fire sanctioned the banning of the German Communist Party; in March, the Enabling Act installed permanent 'emergency powers'; in April, Jews were banned from public office, sports clubs and other institutions, and a campaign against Jewish businesses was launched; in May, the German trade unions were liquidated; in July, other political parties were banned and compulsory sterilisation on eugenic principles was established. There were many other measures.

However, Heidegger resigned the Rectorship in April 1934 and the flow of pro-Nazi speeches petered out.

Careerism and Conformity

Overall, the facts might not seem far removed from Walter Biemel's picture of a short-lived, philosophically insignificant error. It was a politically-charged time. Many people misread the Party, some of its trajectories were not clear and even the Party leaders did not know how far they could go. It was a temporary career compromise – in 1944, Jean-Paul Sartre attributed it to fear, careerism and conformity – and if scarcely laudable it was perhaps understandable in the context of the times. An attendant question: 'how would *we* have responded?'

Heidegger's own version of events was offered to the university authorities in 1945, and again to the weekly news magazine *Der Spiegel* in 1966.[6] He was pressured into the job; and if he did believe in a new German dawn, it was not the same dawn as the one ushered in by the Party. He quickly recognised his mistake. Often, he disagreed with the Party and operated in resistance to Party demands.

That, more or less, is the official story. But it remains puzzling how Heidegger, with a remarkable assimilative capacity and an extraordinary range of reading in Western thought – including an acquaintance with Marx, Freud, Dilthey, Nietzsche and scientists such as Einstein – could have preserved any simple naïvety in the field of political ideas. And anyway, what was that new German dawn he believed in? Was the belief rooted somewhere in his philosophical work? Did it contain elements that might impel someone into active support for a fascist party?

Informing Traditions

Heidegger's earliest sources do not point strongly towards Nazism. His first concerns were theology – Catholic, then Protestant – and early Greek philosophy. The same can be said of another major influence: the modern philosophy of Edmund Husserl who, at the turn of the century, was promoting phenomenology as a radical alternative to the prevalent Neo-Kantianisms and positivisms. Heidegger's sources were marginally fashionable – there had been late-19th-century revivals of Aristotle and medieval scholasticism, and Husserl's phenomenology was the latest thing – but they are scarcely easy to read as central or necessary to Nazism.

However, some aspects of Heidegger's early work have been drawn into the debates. The arguments centre on *Being and Time*, which in 1927 was his major work and a very surprising event in philosophy.[7]

Being and Time: Displacing Subjectivity

Heidegger's concept of *Dasein*, literally 'being-there', offered a dramatically new way of thinking about human being. Usually this had been couched in terms of 'subjectivity', in vocabularies for instance of man, the self, social agency, intentional will or consciousness.

Husserl, for instance, had taken consciousness as the fundamental category of subjectivity: since everything human beings can know or experience turns up there, it had to be philosophy's ultimate, perfect object and the key to being human.

A problem, though, is that human beings are not disembodied consciousnesses. Certainly they can think, calculate and reason, but they also live and experience the world in practical, everyday ways, with others and historically. Hence Heidegger's dramatic adoption in 1925 of a project which would:

. . . get at the totality of the subject which experiences the world and not to some bloodless thinking thing which merely intends and theoretically thinks the world.[8]

So *Dasein* became Heidegger's term for that 'totality of the subject'. In 1927 he offered analyses of *Dasein*'s ways of being, in its 'world' of practical entities (networks of tools and so forth), its attendant moods or dispositions, its adoptions from time to time of observing, calculating or reflective

16

stances. He also analysed *Dasein*'s being 'with others', and in time.

This was philosophically combative. It firmly resisted empiricisms and rationalisms: *Dasein* was not an observable, measurable biological body or a zoological species, nor could it be rationalised as a disembodied mind or consciousness. In Heidegger's loaded terms, it came *before* any of these; it was more fundamental, more 'primordial' or original. It was what had to be there, before any observing or rationalising could get going.

Ontological Knowledge

Heidegger's interest went beyond human being. He asked his readers to question being 'in general', since by 1927 everyone had forgotten to do this.

He had to make a distinction. First, we know that there are entities, or beings, and of many different kinds, occurring to us in many different arenas and conjunctions – a stone, perhaps, two houses, three ruins, four ditch-diggers, a garden, some flowers, a racoon and, of course, reveries and revolutions and much else. Any list of examples will seem absurd. Existing entities and their characteristics are studied and known in 'ontic' knowledges.

Being had to be approached differently. To speak

of the *being of* those entities, the almost indescribable fact that they have their existence, requires 'ontological' knowledge. If Western science and most philosophy were concerned with the ontic, Heidegger privileged the ontological.

There are some consequences for politics, or at least for philosophical discourse on the political. For Heidegger, merely ontic knowledges were less worthy of attention. Out go biology, psychology, economics, anthropology and all their cousins. The world of politics as normally understood, involving empirical information, calculations, facts and so on, would seem to belong to the ontically studied realm. Hence a reserve towards politics seems in order – at least from Heidegger's perspectives in 1927.

An Existentialist Vocabulary

To describe *Dasein*'s ways of being, Heidegger adopted terms from the Danish philosopher Søren Kierkegaard's existentialism. Could this, then, have opened his thinking towards Nazism?

The most telling terms describe how each *Dasein* is unique, and can have its being in two ways: authentically or inauthentically. In its uniqueness, *Dasein* is 'always mine', and 'mine alone'. It is 'the entity that we each ourselves are, which each of us finds in the fundamental assertion: *I am*.[9]

However, *Dasein* can forget this uniqueness, lose it or dissolve it away into the average everyday world, into current preoccupations ('being a stockbroker') and into the ways that everyone else lives ('how They do it'). It becomes inauthentic, scattered and dissipated. The authentic ability-to-be arrives with an anxiety or *angst*, in which *Dasein* is impelled to answer an inner call to recognise the unique wholeness of its being. That includes especially its being within the time-horizon of its own death. This might not sound specifically Nazist, but in some quarters suspicions have arisen.

Adorno and Marxist Critiques

If anyone in the 1950s through to the 1970s wanted both a philosophical and a political critique of Heidegger's work, the most vociferous contenders – though not the only ones – were continental Marxists. They included (among others) Jürgen Habermas in 1953, Georg Lukács in 1953, Theodor W. Adorno in 1964 and Pierre Bourdieu in 1975.[10]

It was Adorno's *The Jargon of Authenticity* that set most of the hares running. It offered a critique of

German existentialist discourse in general, pre-war and post-war, in philosophy, literature and popular culture. Effectively, the 'jargon' of unique, individualised, essentialised human being, with its appeals to authentic experience, was indeed an informing strand of Nazism and had not disappeared in the reactionary, anti-Communist Germany of the Cold War. The jargon connected the two eras and contributed in both to authoritarian social domination. Hidden fascism, in the democracy of the 1960s.

However, it was actually quite difficult to convict Heidegger of all of this. He was primarily an ontologist, not an existentialist. Adorno's most telling point is that the unique 'mine-ness' of *Dasein* prevents any vision of the social except in negative terms: in being-with-others, *Dasein* becomes inauthentic. There are other criticisms: Heidegger turns away from ontic knowledges, like those of economics and politics, while these are necessary to resist fascism. And Heidegger's ontological discourse works by hypnotic assertion, unassailable by empirical evidences or reasoned argument.[11]

These are forceful criticisms, and versions of them crop up in many of the debates. Do they, though, suggest that *Being and Time* carried any commitment specifically to Nazism? Some at least have not read it that way. It was hugely influential on 20th-century existentialisms, which included non- and anti-Nazist thinkers such as Jean-Paul Sartre and Maurice Merleau-Ponty, both men of the Left, both committed Marxists. And more recently, for example, Julian Young has soundly exonerated it of any complicity – *Dasein* in its unique authenticity runs completely counter to Nazi regimentation.[12]

If that is even partly plausible, something must have happened, in Heidegger's thinking or in the sphere of relations of philosophy and politics, between 1927 and 1933. For the moment, a specu-lation: if, in 1927, politics seemed merely ontic or bound into the inauthentic everyday world, might some properly ontological dimension yet be found – something more fundamental that most people could not see or had forgotten? Could someone do with politics what Heidegger had done with *Dasein* – that is, elicit its forgotten, underlying truths, available only to ontological thinking?

It is not clear that that is exactly what happened. But to trace out the encounter, we need to turn back to the Rectorship. The stubborn indelibility of its evidences has not allowed Heidegger's supporters to rest easily.

New Excavations

The official story has been severely tested, if not demolished, by research that appeared in the later 1980s. Documentary evidence had been accumulating in some circles for several decades, especially in Germany and France – for instance, with Guido Schneeberger's publication of the Rectorial speeches in 1962. But the most recent debates were provoked in a few years around 1987. They arrived with research by Victor Farías, Otto Pöggeler and, in the most substantial account, by Freiburg historian Hugo Ott in 1988.[13] Since then, other writers have added to the documentary picture and to its publicity, including Rüdiger Safranski in 1994 with the only extended biography to date.[14] For many of these writers, the official story was a massive, bewitching cover-up.

Commitment to the Revolution

According to the evidence now available, Heidegger's political engagement was no untoward accident. He used the Rectorship as a platform for an explicit, energetic foray into the political arena. It left little room for doubts. The agenda he approved for his inauguration as Rector on 27 May 1933 – attended by the newly-appointed Nazi Minister for Education and Culture, Party officials and military representatives – included a Brahms overture, Nazi flags and the singing of the Party anthem, *Horst Wessel*, with attendant Nazi salutes and shouts of 'Sieg Heil!'.[15] The orchestration of cultural symbols identified Heidegger's Rectorship with the National Socialist revolution from the outset.

His speeches from 1933 to 1934 were radically exhortatory. Addressing six hundred unemployed Freiburg workers drafted into the National Socialist 'labour service' in January 1934, he called for a 'will' to bridge mental and manual labour, a will exalted to a high status:

This will . . . must be our innermost certainty and never-faltering faith. For what this will wills, we are only following the towering will of our Führer. To be his loyal followers means: to will that the German people shall find again, as a people of labour, its organic unity, its simple dignity, and its true strength; and that, as a state of labour, it shall secure for itself permanence and greatness. To the man of this unprecedented will, to our Führer Adolf Hitler – a three-fold 'Sieg Heil!'.[16]

The address to 'German Students', November 1933, stated the following:

The National Socialist revolution is bringing about the total transformation of our German existence [Dasein]. In these events, it is up to you to remain the ones who always urge on and who are always ready, the ones who never yield and who always grow. . . . You are obligated to know and act together in the creation of the future university of the German spirit. . . . Let your loyalty and will to follow be daily and hourly strengthened. Let your courage grow without ceasing so that you will be able to make the sacrifices necessary to save the essence of our Volk and to elevate its innermost strength in the State. Heil Hitler![17]

There is much more in this vein: loyalty, sacrifice, obligation, resolve, and decision, for National Socialism, for the Führer.

In Step with the Party

Most of Heidegger's speeches took contexts and occasions into account. He commemorated the death in 1923 of 'Nazi martyr' Albert Schlageter, a member of the right-wing Free Corps Heinz group of paramilitary saboteurs in the French-occupied Ruhr. Heidegger praised his ability to 'envision what was greatest and most remote', and the qualities of 'hardness of will and clarity of heart', attributing the latter to 'the Alemannic countryside' and 'the autumn sun of the Black Forest'.[18]

He also supported specific policies, such as Hitler's bid to withdraw Germany from the League of Nations, and the Labour Service programme. In fact for Heidegger, steeped by early training in medieval conceits, 'labour' was a category to be made meaningful by coupling it to military service and education, in a united 'threefold bonding'. This organised a bellicose, militaristic discourse on education.

University study must again become a risk, not a refuge for the cowardly. Whoever does not survive the battle, lies where he falls. The new courage must accustom itself to steadfastness, for the battle . . . will continue for a long time. It will be fought out of the strengths of the New Reich that Chancellor Hitler will bring to reality. A hardened race with no thought of self must fight this battle, a race that lives from constant testing . . . [19]

Unsurprisingly, some Heidegger scholars have been taken aback by such discourse, especially when coupled to other evidences. John Caputo remarked in 1993 that '[texts] I had been reading for a quarter of a century suddenly and painfully took on a new and ominous significance'.[20] It also surprised many close associates at the time, both for the energy of its commitment and its choice of political trajectory. In June 1933, Heidegger's closest intellectual ally, the philosopher Karl Jaspers, reported him 'like a man intoxicated, with something threatening emanating from him'.[21]

National Socialist Education

Heidegger seems to have given little or no warning of commitment to National Socialism, or to any political party, before late 1931. He was then reported to be 'following' his wife Elfride into becoming a Party supporter.[22] However, he had entertained notions of a party-politically unspecific national deliverance, shared with other philosophical radicals of the time. In 1918, he conjectured in a private letter to close friend Elisabeth Blochmann:

What shape life generally will assume . . . is uncertain. Certain and unshakeable is the challenge to all truly spiritual persons not to weaken at this particular moment but to grasp resolute leadership and to educate the nation towards truthfulness and a genuine valuation of the genuine assets of existence.[23]

In 1933, the moment to 'educate the nation' seemed to have arrived. His ambitions were far more than local. He took on the self-image of a – or more likely *the* – 'spiritual leader' of National Socialist education.

Bidding to make Freiburg an advance post of that education, he assisted in the drafting of the Baden local legislation which terminated democratic elections for Rectorships.[24] In 1933, ranked against what he saw as a conservative old-guard of university professors, he joined a Nazi coalition forcing the resignation of the board of the German Academics' Association, the official representative body of university teachers, later calling for the Association's abolition.

On a wider scale, he formed alliances with radical Party educational reformers, such as Alfred Baeumler (connected with Alfred Rosenberg's national office for intellectual and ideological education) and Ernst Krieck (a populist of peasant origins), discussing with them the reformation of German universities on Nazi principles.

For Heidegger, this implied radical curriculum reforms: disintegration of the old humanistic disciplines, and regrounding of all human and natural sciences in philosophy as the pre-eminent field. It also meant experiments in a *völkisch* education (see

p. 34) that allied the models of summer camps and hiking holidays – with their attendant virtues of militarism, heroism, masculinism and leadership – to philosophical contemplation. He actually ran one: a *Wissenchaftlager* near Todtnauberg in October 1933, for which SA (*Sturmabteilung*) or SS (*Schutzstaffel*) uniforms were to be worn by their members. 'The goal of the university revolution', he wrote to a participant, 'is the SA student'.[25]

Although some of these early Party alliances fell apart in 1934, Heidegger retained supporters in the Nazi hierarchy until the end of the war, and until at least 1935 he took part in other initiatives at a national level.

In 1934 he joined a committee of the Academy for German Law, pledged by its chairman to operate as a 'fighting committee of National Socialism', reviewing German law in the light of the 'revolution' of 'race, state, Führer, authority, faith, land and idealism'.[26] Neither this profiling, nor the co-membership of notorious anti-Semitist Julius Streicher, seem to have deterred him.

Looking ahead, beyond the end of his Rectorship, in the autumn of 1934 Heidegger volunteered a working plan for the Party's proposed *Dozentenakademie*, an élite national centre for post-graduate education for university teachers – a sphere no longer to be left to the universities but centralised to ensure Party control. This was part of formalised Party strategies; Hitler had presaged such moves in his publication *Mein Kampf*.

The movement disposes of the . . . financial means for the training . . . of minds capable of future leadership. It then distributes the material thus acquired . . . according to criteria of tactical and other expediency.[27]

As a candidate for the leadership of this academy, Heidegger, with poker-faced seriousness, specified for its curriculum 'scientific work, relaxation, contemplation, war games, physical work, marches, sport and festivities'. *Could* this have emerged, at the very best, as fascism in the guise of an administered Dadaism, condemned never to recognise itself? A fool's paradise with a real hell at its heels?

There are laughters of different kinds, including those solicited by the Nazi exhibitions of 'degenerate' art and music – pathological, decomposing, un-German – which began in 1933. We do not know Heidegger's reactions, if any. But we do know his famous valorisation in 1935 of a painting of shoes by Van Gogh, and even in this choice he had conformed to acceptable Nazist taste: it just happened to be the marginal taste for elected 'honorary-Nordic' or 'primitivist' modernists supported, at least until 1936, by Goebbels.[28]

Anti-Semitism

Heidegger had an evident belief in the regime and its Führer – 'the right course for Germany', he emphasised to Karl Löwith in Rome in 1936.[29] However, his writings and speeches carry no overt traces of biological racism. In lectures in the mid-1930s, Heidegger spoke against biologically based, eugenic thought. It ran against the grain of his work of the 1920s: *Dasein* was more fundamental, more original, than any such categories.

Biographical evidences offer a mixed picture. He associated with anti-Semites such as Krieck and Baeumler (see p. 27), and his wife Elfride was known for her overt anti-Semitism. He occasionally subscribed to a hostile drawing of distinctions between Germans and Germans who were Jewish. One attempt to assist Jewish staff also announced his belief in 'the need to enforce to the letter the Law on the Re-Establishment of a Permanent Civil Service', the law that banned Jews from public office. In his draft of a military-style 'code of honour' to be applied to his academic staff, he could write, though without specificity, of a need to 'cleanse our ranks of inferior elements and thwart the forces of degeneracy in the future'.[30]

However, there were Jews among his students, colleagues and friends. Husserl (see p. 15) was of Jewish descent, as was Karl Jaspers' wife, and he offered some of them active assistance (including his research assistant and later editor, Werner Brock). Biological racism seems not to have entirely shadowed his three-year-long affair with Jewish student Hannah Arendt, from 1924, nor their post-war acquaintance from 1950. On his own account, he resisted the posting of an anti-Semitic fly-sheet in the university, forbade a book-burning outside its building and protected library books by Jewish writers.

There are other adducements. Over all, Heidegger seems to have held to no 'principled' anti-Semitism. Nor on evidence did he have any 'principled' outrage, anger or even disquiet or questioning when, in 1933, close friends and associates such as Elisabeth Blochmann, Karl Löwith, Husserl and Arendt were deprived of their jobs and forced into exile. Such events seemed to eventuate as merely unfortunate, like catching a cold. While they looked on with degrees of uncertainty, disgust or horror, Heidegger continued to proselytise the revolution.

Heidegger as Author, Texts as Nazist

Given all the evidence, there can be little doubt of Heidegger's Nazi commitment. But are the charges primarily biographical? They do not prove that his philosophical works are Nazist, that they lead towards Nazism directly or indirectly or that they have Nazist effects.

That has been a constant difficulty. It cannot easily be removed, because what is at stake is how we read texts. Do we hold that 'external' factors, like an author's life or contexts, will have an influence on a text's characteristics? Or do we make only 'internal' readings, insisting that texts are autonomous of their conditions of production? At their extremes, both views are reductive. The Heidegger debates have seen the extremes, as well as much negotiation between them.

On the 'autonomy' side, several accounts assume that the 'Heidegger' that arises in a reading of a text carrying his name is a complex production and is not simply equatable with the actual person who did the writing. If the latter had proven Nazi affiliations, the former, maybe surprisingly, need not. It is an argument that weighs against commentators, like existence-philosopher Karl Jaspers, who assume that the life and work have a necessary continuity. On a similar trajectory, texts need not be assumed to possess some given, inalienable political character or tendency. Walter Benjamin, for instance, argued in 1935 that texts might *gain* a certain political tendency, but this depends on the circumstances of their distribution and reading.[31] In this view, a text can carry a political charge in one context that it might not have in another. Even inversions and reversals are possible.

Neither of these considerations calls us to exclude 'external' factors. Aspects of actual lives and political practices *can* leave their marks, even in a philosophical text. The problem is trying to identify any such passage, along with what allows it to happen. So some critics, often avoiding biographical arguments, have looked for structural connections between Heidegger's discourse and that of Nazism.

Nazist Discourse: the *Volk* and Labour

There are many arguments, some of them extended, that for instance Heidegger's conception of history played a large part in his political choices or that his conception of time shared with Nazism the paradoxical structure of 'conservative revolution' (the radically new future will be made by returning to a lost past).[32]

More commonly, Heidegger's discourse has been found to share *motifs* with Nazi rhetoric.[33] There are many such motifs in the Rectorship speeches, but some also occur in his philosophy, long after 1945.

Regarding the speeches, for instance, Heidegger adopted the anti-democratic 'leader-principle' as both a model and a practice of power. He also adopted the figure of the *Volk*, for Nazism a notion of the people as an undivided organic unity, often coupled to an image of unchanging ruralism. His valorisations of 'rootedness', of '*völkisch* learning' and its 'earth-and-blood-bound force', echoed the conservative-populist discourses which Nazism took over from both popular and élite culture.[34]

Heidegger's views on labour integrated with Nazist discourse. Explicitly countering Marxism, he saw economic classes transcended in the singularity of the *Volk*. There would be a single German estate, or *Lebensstand*, unified in so far as everyone in it worked and 'freely submitted' to the State. If the unemployed lacked work, they were not 'capable of existing [*daseinfähig*]' in the State and for the *Volk*.[35] The *Volk* takes on an ontological dimension, and actual social divisions and differences are seen as less fundamental.[36]

Germany

In conformity with many other German philosophers, Heidegger pronounced Germany as *ursprünglich*, primordial, and at the heart of nations, geo-politically central to Europe and the world. For Heidegger, Germany was also the wellspring of a European rebirth, a nation with a unique destiny or world role. He shared in the rhetoric, if not the reasoning, of the organicist-nationalist historian Oswald Spengler's celebrated call to Germany, in 1919, as the last hope. If Germany goes under, all humanity goes under with it, and without hope for any future restoration.

Nationalistic gestures were bound up with language. Heidegger took up the notion of German as a unique, direct bequest from ancient Greek, undefiled by passage through the deforming conduit of Latin. Greek was the primordial language, the most original of Europe, and German had the direct line of descent. This was advantageous, because for

Heidegger the ancient Greeks had not forgotten being. Direct linguistic connection granted Germany a unique national asset: privileged access to the Greek experience of being.[37]

Structural links between Heidegger's philosophy and Nazism do not end with these motifs. There have been other explanations of what might have been going on.

The *Dasein* of the Nation

Heidegger's central early text, *Being and Time*, is again a reference point. Among many others, Jürgen Habermas has argued that Heidegger's political commitment did have a philosophical basis.[38] He collapsed *Dasein* into the German *Dasein*. No longer unique and 'just-mine', it became the national *Dasein*, the being of the German people.

It is as if Heidegger had been trying to locate an 'authentic' being for the German nation. If *Dasein* arrives only as authentic or inauthentic, then why not nations? *Dasein*, struggling for its authenticity, bidding for its truth of itself, becomes the German nation in its struggle for its own true existence, its mission and destiny. It will find its authenticity in the *Volk*, a unique and undivided entity. The scenario also conjures up the inauthentic nations, losing themselves in everyday business, 'chattering' in inauthentic languages.

There is much to support such a reading, even though it is in part a fiction: Heidegger mostly dropped the existentialist vocabulary from his work after 1927, and in the speeches of 1933–34 he uses other terms (for instance, of 'spirit': the existence of the nation is not so much authentic as spiritual). However, it seems certain that Heidegger's philosophy and the destiny of nations were to have the same trajectory.

A Philosophy for National Socialism

Heidegger linked together the question of being, the imperilled historical moment, and the nation. 'Nations', he said in 1935, 'in their greatest movements and traditions, are linked to being'.[39] According to conservative diagnoses, nations faced a dark moment, a crisis-point in history. For Heidegger, rediscovering the question of being would provide the nation with its saving power. The question of being is 'indispensable if the peril of world darkening is to be forestalled and if our nation in the centre of the Western world is to take on its historic mission'.[40]

So Germany will achieve its greatness as the

nation that rediscovers being. Linked to the ancient Greek sources by language, no nation but the German nation was better placed for the task. Thus philosophy finds its role in the national revolution.

We can speak of historical destiny only where an authentic knowledge of things dominates man's existence. And it is philosophy that opens up the paths and perspectives of such knowledge.[41]

The Nazi revolution would work hand-in-hand with philosophy to clear out the old ways of thought:

The whole of German reality has been changed by the National Socialist State, with the result that our whole past way of understanding and thinking must also become different.[42]

In Heidegger's imagination, it seems, the way would be cleared for his own highly idiosyncratic and institutionally marginal philosophy.

Would the German people sign up? He called them to it. Would the National Socialist government? He dealt, he negotiated. Would his academic colleagues, his institutional associates? Karl Jaspers reported him saying, in 1933, that he could not see why there had to be so many philosophy professors in Germany: two or three would be enough.[43]

Radical Nazism

It was in many ways a bizarre construction – a dream of cohesion announced in ontological language, a nation united in the single primordial question of its being: bound together, fascised, in its being which is also, it should be emphasised, a question. This was not 'standard' Nazism, if ever there was such a thing. That is probably why Heidegger spoke in 1933 of the Nazi revolution as 'not merely the assumption of power as it exists presently in the State by another party, a party grown sufficiently large in numbers to be able to do so'. Out go the voting statistics. Properly, the revolution was the 'total transformation of our German existence [*Dasein*]'.[44]

The bid failed. Heidegger resigned the Rectorship and withdrew from overt political activism. Was that a rejection of Nazism? Perhaps not entirely. Several readers, including in different ways Hugo Ott, Rüdiger Safranski and Jacques Derrida, have identified in Heidegger's politics a bid to construct an ideal Nazism, maybe purer, more stringent and more radical than the actually existing version. The resignation is then explainable as Heidegger's response to the Party's failure to recognise that Nazism: they were, in a sense, not radically Nazi enough. The picture is arguable but there is little doubt that Heidegger had a distinctive view of what Nazism should be. It was he who held its fundamental truth, and it lay in the determined resolve towards the essence of being.

What would, or could, any 'Heideggerean Nazism' have been like? It is a monstrous term, perhaps arising in a complete loss of historical or political reality, perhaps an impossibility.

An End of the Affair?

By 1935, Heidegger had given up hope of any immediate philosophical-political revolution. He took on an 'awaiting' stance. In his 1966 interview with *Der Spiegel*, he declared that if his thinking 'has an effect' in the world, he does not know how. And, he says, any effect may take three hundred years. Nor is it his problem:

I know of no paths to the immediate transformation of the present situation of the world. . . . [I]t would be contrary to the meaning of the task of thought to step up publicly, as it were, to preach and to impose moral judgement.[45]

Heidegger's later philosophical self-image became bound up with an image of the poet Hölderlin, shadowing the Romantic-mystic figure of the solitary seer, 'he who comes first and alone'. It was a qualified return on the leader-figure, which came under his scrutiny before the end of the war for its associations with technical, planning calculation.

He took on twin tasks: pursuing the question of being, in which modern 'planetary technology' figured as a major obstacle, and displacing the received metaphysical foundations of philosophy. He offered to being a thinking couched in terms of eventuation, presence, gathering or mutual co-presencing, and as granted with language, 'keeping' or 'holding' beings.[46] Western metaphysics encountered poetry, medieval mysticism, non-Western philosophies, the Greek Pre-Socratics and other non-standard sources.[47]

And what of Nazism? His texts evaded explicit connection to politics. He did criticise the Nazi regime for its 'technological' bias, and he has much to say elsewhere about how technology has forgotten its roots in *techne* and the Greek experience of being.[48] That has given 'deep' ecological politics, and some other thinking, an extensive resource. But from some perspectives, Heidegger had taken up a typically conservative position. If true to itself, philosophy will deal only with the great, essential questions, beyond immediate historical concerns, beyond mere politics. Otherwise, it is debased, misunderstood or misused.

So Heidegger maintained a strict reticence on the Nazi period. In 1945, with Freiburg occupied by French troops, he was placed under suspension, subjected to de-Nazification proceedings, eventually in 1949 judged a 'fellow traveller' and banned from teaching until 1951.

In many views, the balance sheet has been irredeemably slated against him by that post-war reticence, or silence. For the Nazi regime, its masculinist and militarising programmes, its exclusionary social trajectories, its subjugating operations of power and its racist forced-labour and extermination policies: no anger, no regret, no word of concern.

Reading Heidegger Now

Should, then, Heidegger's texts be safely embargoed? Critics might have to wait for that pleasure. It is not only that the life and work have points of separation. Rather more strongly, Heidegger's thinking might offer *resistance* to Nazisms, indeed to all totalitarian discourse and practices.

The conundrum is not a new one. Sartre, for instance, had dealt with it. He thought an 'existential' politics could be, as he put it, diametrically opposed to Nazism. He wrote in defence of Heidegger's thinking, though not of Heidegger, in a pro-Communist newspaper in 1944:

If we discover our own thought in relation to that of another philosopher, if we ask it for techniques and methods with which we gain access to new problems, does that mean that we espouse all its theories? Marx borrowed his dialectic from Hegel. Will you say that Capital *is a Prussian work?*[49]

Sartre's defences of reading Heidegger are quickly recognisable. We do not have to agree with all aspects of someone's thinking, and an author's avowed politics (including over-fondness for the Prussian monarchy) need not pervade their entire works.

However, whether an opposition to Nazism is so easily gained, or even if it is best to think in terms of 'opposition', now looks more arguable. Those questions have been explored in recent debates.

Heidegger/Post-Structuralisms

Heidegger's influence in post-structuralist thinking is uneven and difficult to chart, but there is not much sign of a Nazi contagion passing around.

For instance, Gilles Deleuze's early counter-philosophy, though prominently Nietzschean, owes much to Heidegger in its de-settling treatment of concept-formation, difference and questioning. And Deleuze's politics owes most to currents of leftist-socialism. Michel Foucault wrote trenchantly against fascism in his preface to Deleuze and Guattari's *Anti-Oedipus*, and in the 1960s his critical rejection of humanist categories of knowledge followed paths that Heidegger opened. In the 1940s and 50s, Jacques Lacan drew from Heidegger's thinking, playing off an ontological conception of language against Saussure's structuralism. Heideggerean terms, for instance of time, enter his descriptions of the psychoanalytic subject: it is temporal, in process, never yet all there. And Lacan's key notion of the Real (recalcitrant to language, not directly knowable, coming before any 'subjectivity') owes much to Heidegger's thinking on being.

Such work has political entailments that are complex, but that has not prevented its use in avowedly Left political arenas – in anti-psychiatry movements, feminist discourses, queer theory and so on.

The conundrum of a Heideggerean thinking in resistance to Nazisms has been addressed probably most closely by Jacques Derrida. It stands as the most dramatic case for re-reading Heidegger, even making him into a contributor to an as-yet-unthought politics of democracy and justice. It asks us, though, to rethink 'politics', 'democracy' and 'justice': those words might have to lose their assurance. So the case is worth exploring in some detail.

The Violence of a Condemnation

Derrida offers a thinking on condemnation and on what Nazism was. First, is Heidegger's Nazism to be condemned? Derrida insists that condemnation of Nazism is not thinking on Nazism. Heidegger, then, might seem to be heading for an acquittal with costs.

In *Of Spirit: Heidegger and the Question* (1987), Derrida emphasises rather than diminishes the 'monstrosity', the 'disastrousness', of Heidegger's Nazism.[50] He states elsewhere the 'necessity of exposing, limitlessly if possible, the profound adherence of the Heideggerean text (writings and acts) to the possibility and the reality of all Nazisms'.[51] And, Derrida has said, he has always condemned Nazism, 'in the horror of what, in Heidegger precisely, and so many others, in Germany or elsewhere, has ever been able to give in to it'.[52] On this one hand, Derrida is unequivocal and emphatic.

However, Heidegger's thinking is not to be rejected. Rather, it can be put to work, for instance, on Heidegger's Nazism. We deal here with another hand, another concern.

Derrida's 'deconstruction' takes up Heidegger's 'overcoming' of Western metaphysics, seeking to disturb, disrupt or destabilise philosophy's foundational concepts, methods, procedures and projects. Necessarily, for Derrida, it is that destabilising thinking that has to be brought to bear on Heidegger's politics. How is this to be done?

Deconstructive Strategies

Metaphysical thought tries to construct an assured distinction of *territories*, of rigorously demarcated fields, spheres, areas and terrains. Politics will not run over into philosophy, what is assuredly Left will be set apart from the Right – we will know with assurance what, and where, things are. Deconstruction insists on *contaminations*, running over and unsettling the borders.

Metaphysical thinking is also *oppositional* thinking: setting something *against* something else, x against y, truth against error, totalitarianism against democracy and so on. That again allows a conceptual certainty: we can make a decision, one term or the other. Deconstruction finds, and plays up, terms or figures that do not fit squarely into those oppositions and which are disruptively undecidable.

So these Heidegger-inspired devices – contaminations, suspicion against oppositions and suspensions of decision – will inform the thinking put to work on Heidegger's Nazism.

'This vile, yet overdetermined thing . . .'

We are playing a dangerous game. Derrida's thinking throws settled concepts into deconstructive movement, rendering them unfamiliar and depriving them of their conceptual authority.

The problem could be put like this. If our thought of 'Nazism' were one of those settled concepts, how could we locate something familiar to condemn? If it were deprived of its conceptual authority, its usual assured sense, then how could we know for sure *what it is* that we are dealing with?

Yet Derrida actively encourages that destabilisation. Assured thought of Nazism is to be unsettled.

It should not be classified 'according to well-known and finally reassuring schemas'.[53] It is not a thing-out-there, carefully segregated from whatever is taken to surround it. Derrida sees more a 'complex and unstable knot', with Nazist and anti-Nazist discourses arriving entwined, perhaps sharing in their traits, maybe operating in a supportive, if sometimes unwitting, network of complicity. So Nazism is thought in terms of contamination: it pollutes, is polluted, and no metaphysically established strategy of demarcation holds it, absolutely. Thus a rather dramatic claim: we do not know what Nazism was.[54]

Beyond Boundaries

Derrida's claim might seem strange, given the weight of historical, social, psychoanalytic, political, economic and other analyses now on offer. However, even empirically orientated studies have confronted difficulties with Nazism as a category. For instance, some recent cultural and social histories have pointed to the 'normalities' and 'ordinarinesses' of life (for some) in the National Socialist period, looking at the continuities as well as ruptures in social, cultural and family relations beyond, through and in advance of Nazism. Other studies have explored how gender and social class inflected meanings and experiences.[55] 'Life in Nazi Germany' was not the same all the way through, and the meanings and experiences do not belong only to one carefully bordered time and place. The inquiries keep producing excesses, not quite containable within the usual categorical boundaries.[56]

Once again, the game can be dangerous. Does this in a peculiar way 'familiarise' Nazism, making it look somehow the same as other regimes, in order even to evacuate its crimes? It could be an apologistic line of argument: Nazism was not the only case, and anyway the economy improved, the trains ran on time. The danger on the other hand is to bundle Nazism safely away, as if it could be immobilised under a demonised name, behind an image-parade titled 'evil' that we all know how to read.

The problem is how to disrupt comfortable determinations, but in a bid for a thinking that can better resist Nazisms. If we take up Derrida's paths, that thinking might not be familiar. Recalling his twin concerns – to condemn and to think – they seem paradoxical. How to condemn Nazism, now and unequivocally, yet insist on pausing while we think on what Nazism was? As Derrida sees it, for Heideggereans there is no rule to decide. They suffer. Their condition is double, having to condemn and think, to judge now and wait while questioning, in a radically discomforting oscillation.

Nazism and Metaphysics

That is a little, more or less, how Derrida, using Heidegger, reads Heidegger and Nazism: there is a condemnation and a thinking. The latter tries to find the still surviving metaphysical residues in Heidegger's texts, and destabilise them. That is the trajectory, or the play, of the readings in *Of Spirit*.

Derrida notes that Heidegger's Rectorial Address of 1933 has a programme, and if it 'seems diabolical', it is because there are two evils at once: a sanctioning of Nazism and a still metaphysical gesture. They take on some couplings.[57]

In 1933, Heidegger adopted the term 'spirit', with rhetorical force (Germany was to have its 'spiritual renewal' and so forth). Given a pragmatic and voluntaristic treatment, the term took on a metaphysical cast, later distrusted by Heidegger. That limited his own earlier deconstructive tendencies and launched the term into the embrace of Nazi rhetoric.

Heidegger's treatment of the word in the 1950s, however, offered it a more deconstructive potential – which Derrida exploits, in an unsettling, debordering play of the kind for which he is well-known. Taking up words of spirit, he entwines with *Geist*, familiar to German speakers, and *spiritus*, lodged in the Latin languages, the Hebrew *ruah* – and also *ruah raa*, 'evil spirit'. Opposition of German to Latin, with a privilege to the former (as with Heidegger), is not allowed to remain stable.

Objections to such readings have arrived rapidly: this is word-play, deflecting attention from the 'important political' issues. Derrida seems to want it both ways, condemning Heidegger while trying to exonerate him; and the condemnation wrestles uncomfortably with the thinking. All of these are probably correct. It is just that for deconstruction, the disruption of metaphysical thinking is necessary to a disruption of Nazist discourse: not simply opposing it head on, but trying to 'unfix' its conceptual foundations.

It might be a powerful suggestion, but some problems remain. Does deconstruction also disrupt all the ethical grounds for condemning Nazism? If it does, how can Derrida or anyone else still condemn it? This has been crucial for attempts to assess the contribution of deconstruction to contemporary politics.

A Heideggerean Ethics?

The question of ethics was not unknown at Freiburg. In 1946, Heidegger set out his differences from Sartre's existentialism.[58] The issue was humanism: taking 'man' as central. For Heidegger, what was first, primordial and properly worthy of thinking, was being. Human beings have to be thought in their relation to being. Effectively, being comes first, human beings second.

To many readers, this has seemed like a desertion of any possibility of ethical judgement. It displaced the *site* of ethics: man, the subject and object of the humane. Heidegger is laid open to charges that, as Jürgen Habermas puts it, he makes man as the neighbour of being more worthy of thought than man as the neighbour of man. In a history scarred by genocide, that has a powerful resonance.[59]

In the same text, though, Heidegger does suggest that he did not defend the inhumane or glorify 'barbaric brutality' or pronounce everything value-less. A desire will necessarily arise for 'rules that say how man should live in a fitting manner':

Should we not safeguard and secure the existing bonds even if they hold human beings together ever so tenuously and merely for the present? Certainly.[60]

One problem: Heidegger's thinking was scarcely going to debate the rules, still less provide any. The concern of thinking is being. So if there are rules, where do they come from? Established authorities, the church and the state, maybe the Nazi state, unquestioned? How can we deal with these rules?

At points like this, Heidegger's friends as well as foes have been tempted to think on his life. His political example is deplorable. And on the few occasions when he breached his post-war silence, out have come his most notorious comments on barbarism and brutality: mechanised agriculture is in essence the same kind of thing as the manufacturing of corpses in gas chambers; the Holocaust was equatable as a phenomenon to the expulsion of Germans from the Baltic states; mass death from starvation (in China) is 'inauthentic' death; and if the post-war housing shortage was causing widespread human immiseration, people need first to note that their real misery is forgetting to think on being.

The History of Being

Heidegger's 'history of being' might be connectable to these statements. The eventuations, the uncon-cealings, the mutual happenings-together, grantings and vouchsafings of being (as he described them) were held to have a history, a performance of themselves across time, in which being itself was in gradual withdrawal. It looks, as Richard Rorty has suggested, like a golden moment for the more-than-ancient Greek Pre-Socratics, or perhaps a little further back, and then a downhill slide all the way.[61] And this was especially marked in the modern, technological age, in which being cannot eventuate in the 'more primordial' ways known to the ancient Greeks.

With such a scenario, Heidegger could lay his own actions at the door of being: it was not so much what *he* did, but how being eventuated itself in him. And it could also allow his seeming insouciance towards the persisting mass horrors and immiserations of the 20th century. On a cosmic scale of Heidegger's kind, these were merely tiny eventuations within the magisterial process of the history of being. He could be quite explicit about this. In 1955 he stated:

The need is for the truth of being to be preserved, whatever may happen to human beings and to all beings.[62]

And speaking of Heraclitus' essential 'strife' of being, that which 'lets gods and humans, freemen and slaves, appear in their respective essence', he comments:

Compared to this encounter, world wars remain superficial. They are less and less capable of deciding anything the more technological their armaments.[63]

Heidegger and Levinas

Could there be any hope of a Heideggerean ethics? Derrida finds in his anti-humanism a useful gesture. It displaces subjectivity, as usually thought, from centrality. In that gesture, some metaphysical absolutes are also displaced (man, the self, consciousness, the subject, the object, right, truth, a certain determination of freedom or of the spirit, or of conscience: Derrida's list).[64]

That might be fine for 'destabilising metaphysics', but it might also sound uncomfortably like Heidegger *redux*, and unpromising for ethics.

However, Derrida's thinking on ethics owes less to Heidegger than to Emmanuel Levinas, of Lithuanian Jewish parentage, domiciled in Paris in the 1920s and an early but quizzical reader of Heidegger. To understand Derrida's sense of ethical and political responsibility, and how it might contribute to a resistance against Nazisms, we have to pursue this a little.

Levinas in 1929 was deeply influenced by *Being and Time*, and in many ways it supplied crucial openings for his thinking. But for Levinas what comes first, before man, subjectivity and so on, is an ethical relation of one human being to another. To be oneself is to be for the other. Compare Heidegger's *Dasein*, having its being in a unique, if anxious, 'mine-only'.

Responsibility

Levinas's relation is ethical because it involves obligations: responsibility for the other. This is not simply symmetrical. The other comes with a demand, has a claim or a call on us, and is therefore subordinate, as a stranger or as destitute.

To be oneself . . . is to bear the wretchedness and bankruptcy of the other. . . . To be oneself [is] the state of being a hostage.[65]

The demand is exorbitant; it arrives without limits set by social norms or decisions.

So the ethical relation is not something chosen.

We are, in and with it. And it is not equatable with morality or even ethics-in-its-usual-sense: applying moral precepts, choosing commitments, establishing rules, calculating rights. It comes before such things:

It is the setting up of a being which is not for itself, but is for all . . . [66]

Levinas says 'for all', and he does bring in the social realm. It is there that the moral precepts, equality of rights and so on are decided. And curiously, this does limit the exorbitancy of the ethical relation. It introduces *justice*, in Levinas' sense: the setting of limits to the responsibility for the other.

It is a discomforting, contradictory entanglement. Justice has to have its acquaintance with the exorbitant responsibility for the other. If not, it is merely a technique for smoothing out social problems, a managerial technique for sorting and regulating the world. It will not even *approach* justice, properly speaking – it heads, rather, in the opposite direction, away from responsibility. And thus with Nazisms: they will try to level the irregularities and exorbitancy of the ethical relation into a prescribed, idealised social uniformity, or otherwise to obliterate it,

and with it the call of the other and the difference of
the other.

Ethics and Politics in Deconstruction

A certain kind of 'politics' might be suggested here,
but of an unfamiliar order. It emphasises responsibility to the singular demand of the other, and yet it
is always in a strained relation to the necessary but
limiting forces of calculation and rational distribution – such as those which establish rights, for
instance, in international law. Derrida has sketched
out the difficulties of this 'double, contradictory or
conflictual' obligation:

[H]ow is one to, on the one hand, *reaffirm the singularity of the idiom (either national or not), the
rights of minorities, linguistic and cultural difference, and so forth? How is one to resist uniform-
isation, homogenisation, cultural or linguistico-
media levelling, its order of representation and
spectacular profitability?*

That is constantly punctuated by the demands of
organisation, calculation, manageability and decision:

. . . on the other hand, how is one to struggle for all that without sacrificing the most univocal communication possible, translation, information, democratic discussion, and the law of the majority?[67]

How do we decide which hand to play? There is no rule. We suffer. There are only moment-to-moment bids, taking a gamble, as in poker. But for Derrida, both sides have to be kept in play: it is necessary to 'betray as little as possible of one or the other'. So organised struggles, couched oppositionally, will be necessary, indeed sometimes urgent. And they must remain open to the un-rule-governed, excessive movements of responsibility.

Offered to political theory this can sound shockingly unspecific. Derrida advances no programmes, methods, goal-orientations, techniques or the like. What deconstruction offers, rather, is an awareness of the limiting powers and trajectories of the usual political discourses, their turn away from responsibility. And it offers strategies that might punctuate that turn.

Some Open Conclusions

Derrida's case is perhaps the strongest and strangest for a Heidegger-inspired resistance to Nazisms. There have been many criticisms, of course, and among the strongest is the accusation that deconstruction is 'irrationalist', setting itself up to disrupt the resources of Western reason. Since those resources have been held to include the emancipatory discourses of the Enlightenment, it is a politically-barbed criticism.

It is not a new charge, though, and it has been shared with Heidegger. In 1954, Georg Lukács' *The Destruction of Reason* saw 'irrationalist' philosophies, especially Heidegger's, as 'paving the way for Nazism', and Adorno and others have repeated the accusation. In 1988, Jürgen Habermas expressed the anxiety that, as Manfred Frank put it, German students reading French post-structuralisms were 're-absorbing their own irrationalist tradition of the pre-war era'.[68]

Much depends, though, on how high a status is given to the political credentials of reason. In 1962, Adorno himself was among the first to describe the Nazi extermination programmes as rationalist in their planning and operation, and the argument has been developed substantially since then by writers such as Zygmunt Bauman.[69] Discomfortingly, we have to note that Heidegger himself had already pointed to the problems of technocratic thinking within the Party hierarchy.

There have been other problems with the notion of a deconstructive politics, including its unspecificity about practical political programmes, strategies and contexts. If we want or need such things, it seems, we have to look to other discourses, other practices, which will be metaphysically grounded and therefore open to deconstruction. Where calculated decisions *are* needed, deconstruction has seemed able to do little more than insist on the imperative of deferring or disrupting decision.

Those debates have been pursued during the last decade or so, but they had already been informed by the practical political theory of radical reforming Marxists Ernesto Laclau and Chantal Mouffe.[70] In the 1980s, they suggested that it was possible to rethink 'democracy' and 'hegemony' in something like a deconstructive way. Democracy, as they see it, is a radical multiplicity, an unmeasurable plurality of competing voices and practices, with a subversive, egalitarian logic: the elimination of relations of domination and subordination. Nevertheless, this has to be held in tension with hegemony: projects and practices of power-taking. Hegemony is not taken purely pejoratively, since the absence of *any* 'common point of reference', or of 'meanings held in common by different social subjects' would lead to an effective collapse, unravelling or implosion of the social fabric.[71] And that would be equally a danger to democracy as the totalitarian bid for unity.

So Laclau and Mouffe conjure a deconstructive oscillation: a play for democratic multiplicities, but also recognising that multiplicities have to be 'articulated', bound up together in hegemonic moves. It is not necessarily a comforting vision of democracy, and moreover, it is a vision of a 'never-yet'. Condemned to perform as constant, unstable punctuations into hegemonic direction and construction, democracy in turn is hegemonically punctuated, along with all its diverse demands and their attendant marginal, anti-system, negative and disruptive forces. Democracy as such, then, is never something achieved. It is neither fixed state nor established condition. It never happens, as such. Or rather, its way of happening is always, as Derrida puts it, in the temporal mode of the 'to come', always adventitious.

Laclau and Mouffe's debt to Heidegger is indirect, but the debates they have been engaging, without vaunted a-politicism or philosophical passivity towards politics, have been marked by many Heideggerean currents of thinking.[72]

So the phrase 'Heidegger's politics' is likely to be

debated for a while yet. As far as the facts of his political engagement are concerned, they are still incomplete. Much remains unpublished, especially his personal papers. Both the facts and the manner of the engagement will continue to call for interpretation. The more difficult problem, perhaps, is how to assess his work as a contribution – strange as it may sound – to thinking on politics today.

The problem is leaving a small wake of destruction in contemporary thinking, and it is multiply compounded by being folded back over onto the politics of Nazism. That folding is at least one reason why the case is not yet closed.

Notes

1. Ian H. Birchall, 'Prequel to the Heidegger debate: Audry and Sartre', *Radical Philosophy*, 88 (March–April 1998), p. 22.

2. Exemplary instances are Terry Eagleton's 'Marxism Without Marxism' in Michael Sprinker (ed.), *Ghostly Demarcations*, New York and London: Verso, 1999; Gregor McLennan's 'The Enlightenment Project Revisited' in Stuart Hall *et al.* (eds), *Modernity and Its Futures*, Cambridge: Polity Press, 1992; and Jürgen Habermas' *The Philosophical Discourse of Modernity* (1985), Cambridge: Polity Press, 1987, especially chapters 1, 5 and 12.

3. Martin Heidegger, *Existence and Being*, ed. Werner Brock, Chicago: Henry Regnery, 1949.

4. Walter Biemel, *Martin Heidegger: an Illustrated Study* (1973), London: Routledge and Kegan Paul, 1977, p. xii.

5. Jürgen Habermas, 'A Philosophical-Political Profile', in Peter Dews (ed.), *Habermas: Autonomy and Solidarity*, New York and London: Verso, 1986, p. 150.

6. Heidegger, 'Letter to the Rector of Freiburg University, November 4th, 1945', and 'Only a God Can Save Us', in Richard Wolin (ed.), *The Heidegger Controversy: A Critical Reader*, Cambridge, Massachusetts: MIT Press, 1993.

7. Heidegger, *Being and Time* (1927), Oxford: Blackwell, 1962.

8. From Heidegger's 1925 commentary on Dilthey, quoted in John van Buren, *The Young Heidegger*, Bloomington: Indiana University Press, 1994, p. 213.

9. Heidegger, *The Concept of Time* (1924), Oxford: Blackwell, 1992, p. 6.

10. Habermas, 'Martin Heidegger: On the Publication of the Lectures of 1935' (1953), in Wolin, *The Heidegger Controversy*; Georg Lukács, *The Destruction of Reason* (1953), London: The Merlin Press, 1980; Theodor Adorno, *The Jargon of Authenticity* (1964), London: Routledge & Kegan Paul, 1973; Pierre Bourdieu, *The Political Ontology of Martin Heidegger* (1975, rev. 1988), Cambridge: Polity Press, 1991.

11. Adorno, *The Jargon of Authenticity*, p. 93ff.

12. Julian Young, *Heidegger, Philosophy, Nazism*, Cambridge: Cambridge University Press, 1997.

13. Victor Farías, *Heidegger and Nazism* (1987), Philadelphia: Temple University Press, 1989; Otto Pöggeler, *Martin Heidegger's Path of Thinking*, Atlantic Highlands, New Jersey: Humanities Press, 1987; Hugo Ott, *Martin Heidegger: A Political Life* (1988), London: HarperCollins, 1993.

14. Rüdiger Safranski, *Martin Heidegger: Between Good and Evil* (1994), Cambridge, Massachusetts and London: Harvard University Press, 1998.

15. Reported in Hans Sluga, *Heidegger's Crisis: Philosophy and Politics in Nazi Germany*, Cambridge,

Massachusetts and London: Harvard University Press, 1993, p. 2.

16. Heidegger, 'National Socialist Education', in *Der Alemann: Kampfblatt der Nationalsozialisten Oberbadens*, 1 February 1934; in Wolin (ed.), *The Heidegger Controversy*, p. 60.

17. Heidegger, 'German Students', 3 November 1933, Ibid., pp. 46–47.

18. Heidegger, 'Schlageter', 26 May 1933, Ibid., p. 41.

19. Heidegger, 'The University in the New Reich', *Heidelberger Neuste Nachrichten*, 1 July 1933, Ibid., p. 45.

20. John D. Caputo, *Demythologizing Heidegger*, Bloomington: Indiana University Press, 1993, p. 2.

21. Jaspers, quoted in Rüdiger Safranski, *Martin Heidegger*, p. 250.

22. Ibid., p. 226.

23. Ibid., pp. 86–87.

24. Ibid., p. 259.

25. Ibid., p. 263.

26. Ibid., p. 281.

27. Adolf Hitler, *Mein Kampf* (1925), London: Hutchinson, 1969, pp. 316–17.

28. Heidegger, 'The Origin of the Work of Art' (1935), in *Basic Writings*, ed. David Farrell Krell, New York and London: Routledge, 1993.

29. Karl Löwith, 'My Last Meeting with Heidegger in

Rome, 1936', in Wolin (ed.), *The Heidegger Controversy*, p. 142.

30. Safranski, *Martin Heidegger*, p. 253.

31. Walter Benjamin, 'The Author as Producer' (1934), in *Reflections*, New York: Harcourt Brace Jovanovich, 1978.

32. See, for example, Peter Osborne, *The Politics of Time: Modernity and Avant-Garde*, New York and London: Verso, 1995.

33. As investigated for instance by Adorno (1964), Bourdieu (1975), Habermas (1985), Sluga (1993) and Caputo (1993).

34. See Sluga, *Heidegger's Crisis*, p. 141, and Bourdieu, *The Political Ontology of Martin Heidegger*, ch. 1.

35. Heidegger, 'National Socialist Education', in Wolin (ed.), *The Heidegger Controversy*, p. 56.

36. Heidegger, 'Declaration of Support for Adolf Hitler and the National Socialist State', 11 November 1933, Ibid., p. 50.

37. Heidegger, 'The Self-Assertion of the German University', May 1933, Ibid., p. 31.

38. Habermas, *The Philosophical Discourse of Modernity*, ch. 6.

39. Heidegger, *An Introduction to Metaphysics* (1953), New Haven: Yale University Press, 1959, p. 37.

40. Ibid., p. 50.

41. Ibid., p. 10.

42. Heidegger, 'National Socialist Education', in Wolin (ed.), *The Heidegger Controversy*, p. 55.

43. Safranski, *Martin Heidegger*, p. 231.

44. Heidegger, 'Declaration of Support for Adolf Hitler and the National Socialist State', in Wolin (ed.), *The Heidegger Controversy*, p. 52.

45. Heidegger, 'Only a God Can Save Us', Ibid., p. 110.

46. See, for instance, *Poetry, Language, Thought*, New York: Harper and Row, 1971, and *Pathmarks* (1967), Cambridge: Cambridge University Press, 1998.

47. The best single example is Heidegger's *The Principle of Reason* (1957), Bloomington: Indiana University Press, 1996.

48. Heidegger, 'The Question Concerning Technology' (1953), in *Basic Writings*, ed. David Farrell Krell.

49. Sartre, quoted in Birchall, 'Prequel to the Heidegger Debate', p. 24.

50. Jacques Derrida, *Of Spirit: Heidegger and the Question* (1987) Chicago and London: University of Chicago Press, 1989, ch. 5.

51. Derrida, 'Heidegger, the Philosophers' Hell' (1987), in *Points . . . Interviews, 1974–1994*, ed. Elisabeth Weber, Stanford: Stanford University Press, 1995, p. 186.

52. Derrida, 'Comment donner raison?' (1987), Ibid., p. 194.

53. Derrida, 'Heidegger, the Philosophers' Hell', Ibid., p. 186.

54. Ibid., p. 184.

55. Many of these studies have been influenced by the 1980s '*Historikerstreit*' controversy over German history: see, for example, the essays in David F. Crew (ed.), *Nazism and German Society*, New York and London: Routledge, 1994, and Michael Burleigh (ed.), *Confronting the Nazi Past: New Debates on Modern German History*, London: Collins and Brown, 1996.

56. For instance, Linda Schulte-Sasse finds 1930s German cinema to be less 'propaganda' or 'kitsch' than consumer entertainment sharing formulae and pleasures with classic Hollywood film: *Entertaining the Third Reich: Illusions of Wholeness in Nazi Cinema*, Durham and London: Duke University Press, 1996.

57. Derrida, *Of Spirit*, ch. 5, p. 40.

58. Heidegger, 'Letter on Humanism' (1947), in *Basic Writings*, ed. David Farrell Krell.

59. Habermas, 'Work and *Weltanschauung*: the Heidegger Controversy from a German Perspective' (1988), in Hubert Dreyfus and Harrison Hall (eds), *Heidegger: A Critical Reader*, Cambridge, Massachusetts and Oxford: Blackwell, 1992, p. 199.

60. Heidegger, 'Letter on Humanism', in *Basic Writings*, ed. David Farrell Krell, pp. 249–50, 255.

61. Richard Rorty, 'Heidegger, Contingency and Pragmatism', in Dreyfus and Hall, *Heidegger: A Critical Reader*, pp. 209–17.

62. Heidegger, 'On the Question of Being' (1955), in *Pathmarks*, p. 236.

63. Ibid., p. 321.

64. Derrida, 'Comment donner raison?', in *Points . . .*, p. 194.

65. Emmanuel Levinas, 'Substitution' (1968), in Seán Hand (ed.), *The Levinas Reader*, Cambridge, Massachusetts and Oxford: Blackwell, 1989, p. 107.

66. Ibid., p. 106.

67. Derrida, 'A "Madness" Must Watch Over Thinking', (1991), in *Points . . .*, p. 360.

68. Habermas, 'Work and *Weltanschauung*', in *Heidegger: A Critical Reader*, op. cit., p. 189.

69. Zygmunt Bauman, *Modernity and the Holocaust*, Cambridge: Polity Press, 1989.

70. Ernesto Laclau and Chantal Mouffe, *Hegemony and Socialist Strategy: Towards a Radical Democratic Politics*, New York and London: Verso, 1985.

71. Ibid., pp. 187, 188.

72. For discussions of the issues see Simon Critchley, *The Ethics of Deconstruction: Derrida and Levinas*, Cambridge, Massachusetts and Oxford: Blackwell, 1992, ch. 5, and Richard Beardsworth, *Derrida and the Political*, New York and London: Routledge, 1996.

Further Reading

John D. Caputo and Jacques Derrida, *Deconstruction in a Nutshell: a Conversation with Jacques Derrida*, Fordham University Press, New York, 1997.

Jacques Derrida, *Politics of Friendship* (1994), Verso, New York and London, 1997.

Luc Ferry and Alain Renault, *Heidegger and Modernity* (1988), University of Chicago Press, Chicago and London, 1990.

Philippe Lacoue-Labarthe, *Heidegger, Art and Politics: the Fiction of the Political* (1987), Blackwell, Oxford, 1990.

Jean-François Lyotard, *Heidegger and 'The Jews'* (1987), University of Minnesota Press, Minneapolis, 1990.

Günter Neske and Emil Kettering (eds), *Heidegger and National Socialism: Questions and Answers*, Paragon Press, New York 1990.

Richard Wolin, *The Politics of Being: The Political Thought of Martin Heidegger*, Columbia University Press, New York, 1990.

Michael E. Zimmerman, *Heidegger's Confrontation with Modernity: Technology, Politics, Art*, Indiana University Press, Bloomington, 1990.

Other titles available in the Postmodern Encounters series from Icon/Totem

Derrida and the End of History
Stuart Sim
ISBN 1 84046 094 6
UK £2.99   USA $7.95

•

What does it mean to proclaim 'the end of history', as several thinkers have done in recent years? Francis Fukuyama, the American political theorist, created a considerable stir in *The End of History and the Last Man* (1992) by claiming that the fall of communism and the triumph of free market liberalism brought an 'end of history' as we know it. Prominent among his critics has been the French philosopher Jacques Derrida, whose *Specters of Marx* (1993) deconstructed the concept of 'the end of history' as an ideological confidence trick, in an effort to salvage the unfinished and ongoing project of democracy.

Derrida and the End of History places Derrida's claim within the context of a wider tradition of 'endist' thought. Derrida's critique of endism is highlighted as one of his most valuable contributions to the postmodern cultural debate – as well as being the most accessible entry to *deconstruction*, the controversial philosophical movement founded by him.

Stuart Sim is Professor of English Studies at the University of Sunderland. The author of several works on critical and cultural theory, he edited *The Icon Critical Dictionary of Postmodern Thought* (1998).

Foucault and Queer Theory
Tamsin Spargo
ISBN 1 84046 092 X
UK £2.99   USA $7.95

Michel Foucault is the most gossiped-about celebrity of
French poststructuralist theory. The homophobic insult
'queer' is now proudly reclaimed by some who once
called themselves lesbian or gay. What is the connection
between the two?

This is a postmodern encounter between Foucault's
theories of sexuality, power and discourse and the
current key exponents of queer thinking who have
adopted, revised and criticised Foucault. Our
understanding of gender, identity, sexuality and cultural
politics will be radically altered in this meeting of
transgressive figures.

Foucault and Queer Theory excels as a brief introduction
to Foucault's compelling ideas and the development of
queer culture with its own outspoken views on
heteronormativity, sado-masochism, performativity,
transgender, the end of gender, liberation-versus-
difference, late capitalism and the impact of AIDS on
theories and practices.

Tamsin Spargo worked as an actor before taking up her
current position as Senior Lecturer in Literary and
Historical Studies at Liverpool John Moores University.
She writes on religious writing, critical and cultural
theory and desire.

Nietzsche and Postmodernism
Dave Robinson
ISBN 1 84046 093 8
UK £2.99   USA $7.95

Friedrich Nietzsche (1844–1900) has exerted a huge
influence on 20th century philosophy and literature – an
influence that looks set to continue into the 21st century.
Nietzsche questioned what it means for us to live in our
modern world. He was an 'anti-philosopher' who
expressed grave reservations about the reliability and
extent of human knowledge. His radical scepticism
disturbs our deepest-held beliefs and values. For these
reasons, Nietzsche casts a 'long shadow' on the complex
cultural and philosophical phenomenon we now call
'postmodernism'.

Nietzsche and Postmodernism explains the key ideas of
this 'Anti-Christ' philosopher. It then provides a clear
account of the central themes of postmodernist thought
exemplified by such thinkers as Derrida, Foucault,
Lyotard and Rorty, and concludes by asking if Nietzsche
can justifiably be called the first great postmodernist.

Dave Robinson has taught philosophy for many years. He
is the author of Icon/Totem's introductory guides to
Philosophy, Ethics and Descartes. He thinks that
Nietzsche is a postmodernist, but he's not sure.

Baudrillard and the Millennium
Christopher Horrocks
ISBN 1 84046 091 1
UK £2.99   USA $7.95

'In a sense, we do not believe in the Year 2000', says French thinker Jean Baudrillard. Still more disturbing is his claim that the millennium might not take place. Baudrillard's analysis of 'Y2K' reveals a repentant culture intent on storing, mourning and laundering its past, and a world from which even the possibility of the 'end of history' has vanished. Yet behind this bleak vision of integrated reality, Baudrillard identifies enigmatic possibilities and perhaps a final ironic twist.

Baudrillard and the Millennium confronts the strategies of this major cultural analyst's encounter with the greatest non-event of the postmodern age, and accounts for the critical censure of Baudrillard's enterprise. Key topics, such as natural catastrophes, the body, 'victim culture', identity and Internet viruses, are discussed in reference to the development of Jean Baudrillard's millenarian thought from the 1980s to the threshold of the Year 2000 – from simulation to disappearance.

Christopher Horrocks is Senior Lecturer in Art History at Kingston University in Surrey. His publications include *Introducing Baudrillard* and *Introducing Foucault*, both published by Icon/Totem. He lives in Tulse Hill, in the south of London.